SY

S

SYMPHONIC SILENCES

Opal V. Oehler

VANTAGE PRESS
New York

Contents

Foreword

For her many friends and devotees, when Opal Virden Oehler finally relented and agreed to submit her favorite poems for publication, it was a very happy day. For years certain friends would receive one of her inspirations as a gift for a special occasion, as a "lift up" during a weighty time or an expression of friendship and caring just when most needed—an uncanny experience. God had gifted Opal with springs of timeless paradigms, yet apt, and meant for each and every moment of time. We would each say, "Surely that poem was meant for me!"

Those who share Opal Virden Oehler's openness to the wiles and wonderfulness of the Holy Spirit, know that it is this Spirit who is permitted to flow through her to minister to those in need of a particular blessing, be it cathartic intervention or confirmation and assurance. Such is the medicine of the inspired poem.

Opal was born in Plainview, Texas, center of the Fertile Hight Plains, in 1908. She received her bachelor of science degree from the University of Houston and a master of education degree from the University of Texas at Austin. During World War II the Army sensed her specialness by appointing her as musical therapist at the rehabilitation center at Fort Knox, Kentucky.

When the war ended she turned down opportunities to advance herself professionally in the metropolitan areas and chose to dedicate herself to the education of tiny children in El Paso and Ozona in West Texas. In 1971 she thought it was time to retire. She married Rudolph Oehler of Fredericksburg. They made their home a few miles into the batholithic, wooded Hillcountry outside of historic Fredericksburg in Central Texas—where she resides today.

Jackrabbits, whitetail deer, armadillos, flying wild turkey, and many other "friends" sense that they are welcome, including the human kind, at her Olive Branch Ranch, which is what she calls their homestead.

As chairman of the heritage committee of the 150th Anniversary of Fredericksburg's founding in 1846, it is with great pleasure and satisfaction that I speak with sincerest gratitude that she is releasing this book during 1996, our jubilee year. We are honored to have this gifted poet among us; and this compendium that will bless not only us, but future generations who will be led to open it at their appointed moments.

Opal's retirement vocation is the organ and the piano. For years, should a pastor be in need, he had only to give Opal a ring and she would happily provide the accompaniment for the singing of hymns at liturgies and prayer meetings. Afterward, she would be "tanked full" again with new inspirations, new themes, and new poems.

This collection of poems was selected by Opal following prayer and hunch, in hopes they might be meaningful and enjoyable to those led to read them for one reason or another. But from long experience, permitting herself to be a vessel, she offers these poems trusting them to be a gift of mystical messages in the phenomena of providential predestination. Not to have shared these poems would have precluded the unique experience they provide to this and future generations, and until time as we know it is delivered into eternity.

—Kenn Knopp
Fredericksburg, Texas
1996

SYMPHONIC SILENCES

Part I

Fellowship with God

Cathedral of Joy

Of need to worship I was fashioned
And given mind akin to light;
Then set in dust with strong compassion
For my starless, empty night.
Then dawn o'erspread the whole creation
And bade me name all things in sight.
Without a moment's hesitation
I named its Author as the height
Of all my urgent aspiration
And gave my love in sheer delight.

My heart is honored now: His temple
Is for us a meeting place
For meditation pure and simple—
I'm now at home before His face—
Altho' I wonder if I might
Come near enough to touch the lace.

The music of my thought serene
O'erflows the sanctuary brow;
Realities in tempered sheen
Light the candles of my vow,
Communion lends new incensed wing
Unto my resurrection now.

A Prayer

God, keep my beloved facing
Toward the East lighted from within
Thy fellowship, all else forsaking.
Promise peace with each day's end.
Hold fast his mind (Thy silvery flute),
Breathe through his thoughts Thy melody
Of achievement—grandly mute
To all but those who comprehend.

Thanks, Lord

Thank You, Lord
For letting me just be
A pool of contentment
Savoring the hovering breezes
Of Your Presence.

Thank You that life
Is the art of Quietude
Just happening inside some strife
While Your grace provides its certitude.

Thank You for alliances
That oversee our coming Home;
The music of Love's silences
That still the heart until full-blown
My-self to Thy-Self can surrender
(While traveling Love's Holy Land)
To the drum-beat of a splendor
Beauty's joy can understand.

The Lord Called

"Look forward,
    Away from all pain,
    Self-pity and sighing
    In selfish disdain."

"Look forward,
    For grace to endure;
    Whatever the future
    Keep the heart pure."

"Look forward,
    Turn every corner of Time
    Arrayed with a rainbow of prayer"
    Loneliness conquers no clime
    Guarded by His sovereign care.

Conclusion

Through swirls of angel-guarded beauty
Your wholeness held my bartering stance
Until my will perceiving duty
Refined the pond'rous avalanche
Of quavering rhymes that minds pursue
To gain the arms of the cross of Truth.

Give Me Grief

Dear God, give me all my grief
Now—to keep my soul against
That day when I should weep
In solitude of growing old
A stranger still to pain's relief.

Mission

God of goodness, Lord of Life,
Lend Thy grace to bear me far
Apart into Thy inner court
Of love. There let me be a star
To guard the lonely distances
That steep the soul in cunning night
Of cold ambition's blight,
Lest unwittingly they might
Not glimpse Reality's
Dear healing light.

Courage

The tide of chance had run far out.
The anchors of the mind were few.
The hope that brinked the edge of doubt
Was not refreshed with morning dew.

On toward Jerusalem somehow
His brave young face was firmly set.
Gethsemane: (tho' hard-by now)
He skirmished there without regret.

Alone! Alone before the cross
Of indecision sore and bare,
He yearned in truth to know the cost
And drank the cup of self-earned prayer.

The chilling sweat of loneliness
Demanded morsels of divine
Recognition then to bless
The newfound image in his mind.

Receptive to divinity
That overshadows ebb and flow,
He savored continuity
With star-lit courage crisp as snow.

Finality

The winnowing wings of longing
Brush away the dross of failure,
Leaving in their surly wake
Star-strewn mysteries of desire
To gaze from off the tallest loft
Of fame:
Feel its bold cold wind carve my name
(E'en in pillared peaks of pain)
To eulogise the stark ascent of soul
Seeking wonderment to make it whole.

Whole? Oh, Dream, arrest this flight of Self!
Fill the cup with sterner stuff of care
Lest too much knowingness despise
The rainbow-altared prayer
Of those who give with lowered eyes
A willing sacrifice
To bless the lame, the rich, the bare.

No templed arch of self can stand
Above those statured by the hand
Of God.

To My Lord

Teach me, O Lord, to ask aright
For Your companionship tonight.
My earthly mirth will never do
To satisfy my heav'nward view
Because You've urged my heart to seek
Eternal glories all this week
Through everyday simplicities
That we might share life's mysteries:
Absolving Time-dust from my eyes,
You bade me savor Paradise.

Devotion In Toto

Wherever he sleeps—the Lord abides there.
Whenever he speaks—'tis the Lord that is heard.
However he weeps—it is our Lord's prayer.
His song is the music to God's holy Word.

Everywhere is his dwelling place.
Wisdom is filling his tenderest plea:
That all mankind might nobly face
Living as God's intended poetry.

Oh, to Be Me

In truest revelation,
God-intended
Free!

Somewhere in the lonely highlands
Of self-revered integrity
are doubts like isolated islands
endangering my will to be.

"Come and see," the stillness calls.
Then a heart-throb locks the door.
Tho' a lostness deftly falls
My heart awaits the call once more.

"Come and see," the Master urges,
"Share my Truth without disguise."
His Word of love in truth converges
Upon my heart and satisfies.

Love in Bloom

Something deeply
Beautiful
Makes of Hope an holy shawl
To warm the leaning shoulders of
Disappointment; and decorate the wall
Of empty hearts whose chilling need
Is just a candle of a prayer
Lighting eyes where heartaches feed
On the gentle glow of instant care.

Spread a broader cloth of kindness
On which to share the bread of laughter;
Watch Beauty candlize a fineness
Proving Love is Evil's master
Resolutions heart to heart
Are bourne to beautify the manger
That birthed on earth the heavenly art
Of unifying Friend and Stranger.

I Believe

I believe
The province of my role to care
In fellowship, as man to man
Is cumbered with a would-be prayer
Caught in the teeth of contradictions
Gaudy with luxuriant fare
So void of chaliced benedictions.

I believe
A Holy Challenger foreknew
My own deep need of clemency—
Believing as He must, He grew
Full-statured in Gethsemane.
Then standing tall to make assent
Unto rebirth of Adam, He
Bare-handed, wrestled God's design
To fill the hungry heart of me
And slake my thirst with Freedom's wine.

The farthest star now vies my thrust
Of this believing—as I must.

Jesus and the Little People

O Blessed Presence, cover them
With holiness of touch to dim
The din of unimportant whim;
Then grant their days love's diadem.

Grant the gentleness of mind
That can open up the heart
To the treasures each can find
When each one takes and gives a part.

By laying down their nets of goals
That did not tell that men are brothers,
And follow Him beyond Life's shoals
To share its deeper joy with others.

A Reality of Christmas

Ere my heart returns to common pride
    in day-to-day employ

Let the mind intent, dissatisfied
    separate alloy

And cherish truth and beauty that abide
    in holy Christmas joy.

Tho' rafters rang with nuisant glee
    while eager children played

Shrilling voices blended perfectly
    (because their hearts were on parade)

Deeming childhood's reciprocity
    dearly unafraid.

Lest angel-footed echoes disappear
    (silent as a kiss)

Down the stairway of my heart I'll hear
    (in memory a tryst)

These revelries become their yester-year
    (as wisdom will insist)

I would that mem'ry grant to them anew
The nuisant glee that kept them free
From grown-up fortune-tainted rue.

In Fellowship with Him

Jesus opens many doors
For my heart's employ:
Blossoming in quiet places of my day.
Just now the fog of envy left me
Leaving room for love to bloom His way.

He redeems my moments when
Otherwise I would've been
Blinded to a blessing only He could send.
I'm always asking His forgiveness;
And inviting Him to share this
Urgency I feel for you
Within the framework of His love
Where inventory candles of
Our thoughts of you combine
In mutuality of mind.

Thank God I dwell in heavenly Now:
Each day is keeper of my vow
To be present to your need
Of a convenated friend
Who kneels for you that He might lead.

An Agape Bloom

You were the Morning Star
Attending my Infancy
Of adolescent dreams
Lost in vacant stares
Of vain Uncertainty

Standing by me through High Noon
Of Dedication's salient Aura
Your Presence clothed my artlessness
With understanding's Rainbow
Nurturing Fulfillment's
Quest

Now the Sunset Ray of Truth
Shares Beauty's fellowship
With Pain to garner
Faith as Love obeys
Death's curtain-calling Drama
Looming just beyond
Time's final *Abend*
Flamme

Brotherly Love

The Master walked awhile with me
Beside the Galilean Sea.
He led me to the peaceful shore
To tell me of the love in store
For all mankind He came to free
With His good news of Calvary.

He told of mountains I must climb
And Sorrow's valleys I must find
To mend a brother's broken will
And share a courage to be still
'Til we receive joy from above;
His mantle of brotherly Love.

A Holy Saturday Meditation

Lord of the Garden, Your heart entombed
God's will inherent, there it bloomed
With strength to win o'er any odd:
Because You were the Son of God.

Lord of the Sorrows along life's way,
The pain of growing attends our day
Of opportunities begun:
Because You acted as God's Son.

Lord of the Anguished (body and mind),
Your quivering flesh was rent to refine
The lottery crowd at the foot of the knoll:
Because You dreamed that Man is whole.

Lord of the Promise: "Today thou shalt be . . . ,"
That promise of Paradise calls now for me.
Untiming Your towering hour of youth:
Your homing heart paused to uncurtain Love's Truth.

Lord of the Silence (that crushes the mind),
Waiting outside of the tomb I can't find
Your travail of hell in a dark of my own:
Because Resurrection recaptured life's song.

Lord of the Morning, this dawn in my heart
(Affirming Your mission in which I've a part)
Sets the winds moving in heavenward tow:
Your Joy is compelling and Love bids me go!

Belonging

I belong, I belong to the Lord
Someone came searching and longing for me,
Then He called my name—my lonely heart came
When He said, "Come and see."

He with gentle hand touched mine,
Speaking promises divine;
Loosing Time-Dust from my eyes
My heart became so newly wise:

In His lingering Presence now it seems
Our fellowship was always there in His dreams!
Now I know I belong to the Lord.

The glint of steel in Jesus' smile
Designs my cross of self-denial
Through Poverty's grey loneliness is heard
His call that I must serve the Bread of His Word!

Blest contentment I share
Here I abide in His care
Oh, this is where I belong
I belong to the Lord.

Reconciliation

Eternity Past foreknew Calvary's Hill
Would echo, "Father, receive Thy Son."
"It is finished! Peace; be still."
Thus God's offertory of Life was sung.
Because the joy of choice was given,
Man must needs to claim its Truth.
Then the fellowship of Heaven
Endows to Man eternal Youth.
Strains from Calvary send His Love
Gliding pillared aisles on earth
Resounding heavenly anthems of
Calvary—cathedral to the Universe.

My High Priest Is

He is a higher priest—
Undisguised by lavish stole:
His thoughts are a richer feast
Than warning. He would make whole
The broken artifice of mankind
And clothe with faith the arid soul,
And guide the feeble to the Mind
Whom to know is to be whole.

Victory

Words may stumble through the mist
    of indecision
Stewing echoes of despair
    that roam the sea of vain derision
But to be silenced by
    the periscope of prayer.

Part II

Fellowship with Nature

Beauty Known

How do we hold the true?
The beautiful?
Or the fragile fleeting gift
Of an instant understanding
Feathering Beauty's wings to lift
The soul above the towering wall of things:
Oh, suddenly the heart's own gift
Of understanding vies with Saturn's rings.

Sweet Tomorrows

Sweet Tomorrows, tho' thou shouldst withhold
The new from me (who am so new to Time),
No lesser melody should claim my rhyme.
For I have Today—
And Yesterday's still as fresh
As thy deeply sleeping rose
Of promise. And my day surely knows
This quietude my loves design—
Whilst Thou, Sweet Morrows, only pine.

Levelness

Dreams are fairy tales—like radar
    Denting frozen walls of Time—
Return as jeweled, frosty vapor
    Obscuring harbors of the mind.

Youth is always fortune-seeking—
    Funded by the lure of age.
Eternality lies weeping
    As an incognito sage.

Resounding through Life's layered canyon
    Are contrapuntal hymns that find
Their leveled solitude companion
    Music to Eternal Mind.

Hills of Music

Unto the hills—among the hills—
Oh, lambent hills of music:
Sentinel of my soul's frontier!
My wingéd, longing being chooses
To station on thy roofless sphere.

Beauty looms o'er thy dimension
In quick'ning chords of cadent life;
Even torrents of derision
(Rhythmed in discordant strife)
Give way to crystallizing bars
Of daring contrapuntal theme
To harmonize the rampant stars
And measure Hope's orchestral dream.

Awake this hymn of Truth in me:
The hills of music haloed in
Divinely fingered harmony
My most elusive joys portend:
While holding captive, set me free!

The Smile of Truth

Oh smiling, sovereign God,
Thy cloned creation
Cries from skies
And clod
For perfect animation
That each will rise
In their own mod
Justifying revelation.

Every liar and orbit gather
Their own honor from Thy smile.
These entities of being feather
Reasons for their own lifestyle.

This holiness of Beauty's treasure
Lies innocently unrehearsed;
God's own heartbeat set the measure
Felt throughout the universe.

To Beauty

Dear Beauty is my god, I said
And vowed to her my will to know
Her rhythmic labyrinth that led
My wistful heart beyond its glow
Of musing. Now I feel
Her grace escape me, tho' I kneel.

A queen in life—tho' not its god—
You most nobly cool the face
Of weariness that must needs plod;
You clothe the mind with jeweled lace.
Most graciously, my heart doth fear
Thy mission is but to endear.

Maturity

Her smile becomes a canopy of grace,
Imposing, solicitous and gay.
Her presence lingers in the secret place,
Forbidding idleness to claim its prey.

An arc of silver hope defines her brow
Made noble in its height of understanding.
To forego the glint of Wisdom's prow
Her eyes are lowered but commanding.

Courage, welling gently sure of righteousness,
Grows like a tree beside the water—
Is drawn from nethersprings of selflessness
To share a proven greater order.

Patience (nourished by a cool conviction
Rooted in the quiet of love,
Acquainted with the dire affliction
Of the dust we're all part of)
Mellows disappointment's crucible,
Changing ashes of refining sorrow
Unto a joy that's usable—
If not now—then some tomorrow.

Moon Talk I

Oh, Man-in-the-Moon, you can see so far!
What do you know about me?
Oh, carve me a name while using the flame
Of the Evening Star I can see.

I've lain so alone on Earth's pillow-stone:
Wandering thoughts shadow me
Feigning to fashion a will of compassion,
Then judgement forecloses on me.

How I'd love to give all the days I will live
On the earth for an orbit with you!
With my humanly mind I would vow to divine
All the mandalas earthlings eschew.

I'd challenge their bent that stirs malcontent
Inciting the millions aflame
With idols much stranger that God in a manger
Denying the Child His own name.

The role of the Child cannot be defiled
By the whimsy or smallness of Man.
This very Child played with planets inlaid
With the gold of His own Father's plan.

Moon Talk II

Humanity grew full-statured when through
The Time-honored space they went
And people out there—(God only knows where),
Revealing their singular tint.

The paradox nursed in our universe
Related the hunter as hunted:
Man cannot rest and God cannot bless
Until they are justly confronted.

For Maker and Man there is but one plan
For enhancing the whole universe:
Acknowledging men to be next of kin,
God came in His Son to disperse

His wonders of Heaven to share as Earth's leaven,
Combining all glories so grand.
Man's heart is re-christened because he has listened
To "Peace and good will toward man."

Hence no other age will further engage
To exploit the mandalac rue.
The Wise have the heart to frame their own art:
Perceiving the Christly is true!

Angel Wing

You were with me
In the breeze that rose
To skirt the lea—
Bidding flower pose
While you sheltered me
In tints of peace that fold
My soul in nurture sweetly new.
Ah—you thought I'd never know
That brush of angel-wing was you.

Dreams Are for Keeps

My satiny saffron pillow
    (Softly billowy deep)
Enshrine my dreams so willowy
    Fragile as your dimpled cheek.

Oh, lay aside all temporal booty
    And its hold of foolishness.
Grant me the onliness of beauty
    Commensurate with holiness.

My heart now harbors one sweet touch:
    A memory of instant care
That gave o'erwhelmingly of such
    Reality that dreamers share.

Part III

Lyrics

My Caravan

Across the sands of white desire
My caravan of Love's own thoughts
Depart the oasis of your presence
To seek the far-most solitudes
Of your beauty
And bear me witness that my heart
Is wise to seek its own.

Constancy

My love is a simple love,
It covers everything:
Quartetting birds that swirl above
My Wint'ry days the same as Spring.

Timidly it flowers blessings
In my moments near despair
To overcome my silly guessings
Whether/If you really care.

My love is simple, everlasting,
And gilds your toughish tenderness
With my heart's continued fasting
Lest it lose Love's holiness.

Rebuke

My hero doesn't need me.
My ship of dreams at anchor lies.
If my beloved goes to sea
I'll roam the shore in weird disguise.

My cross becomes the cloistered nun
But daintier than starry skies
My proud heart dons the frills of fun
O'er royal purple of the wise.

Sweetheart

Dear Heart, I need you for the way
Your quiet eyes look into mine,
And grant my homing soul its day
Of sweet release to heavenly clime.

And soon, perchance, I'll wake to find
That this good you are to me
Is tiered in charities of mind
Flowering immortality.

Remembering

Because you pushed the gates of Now ajar
I see Me standing holding my own star:
This Isle o'Mine God set aside for me:
An holy rhyme that I'm to be.

Within a shell of vain and pond'rous thought
Me-ness surged anew ('gainst pangs of taut
And darkened hordes of labyrinthian schemes),
To gather Truth and feather-lifting wings.

The hov'ring wings of Now endow my peace
Unfettered by traditional retreats.
Through thoughts of you my solitudes indwell
A joy of Truth that youth cannot excel.

Time Is for Being

Time enfolds our days together
Like the petals of a rose.
Fragrance of the mem'ries never
Fails to win the heart repose.

Three hundred sixty-four the days
Have come and gone ten times since then;
The calendar of love displays
Beatitudes that make amends.

A half a million times we've been
As one, a duplicating heart;
When a sorrow sought to win
The oil of faith would heal the smart.

Altho' these years have simply flown
Oblivion can not consume them.
Our days well-listened to their song
Believing God pre-saged and tuned them.

O Sweet Return

I know you have to go
To some quaintly stately foreign affair.
That's all right, but this very night
Quarrelsome omens are plying the air.

You said good-bye, I turned to sigh,
"This month will have more nights than a year."
I watch you departing, it sets my eyes smarting
But I'll hold no fellowship with a tear.

Today is the day all calendars say is "8"*
In silence your promises litter the walk.
You should have heard our pet hummingbird
Whispering pity of me to the tall hollyhock.

Oh? The door stands ajar! I heard no car?
Ah, what 'livens and sweetens my fingertips!
This soul-fest of honey could've come only
From your cautiously love-giving lips.

*You promised to return by September 8.

Sleep

You admit to sleeplessness
    (That coincides with mine, I guess.)
All the blinking stars deplore
    Keeping watch till half-past four.

So from four to five a. mzzy
    Rumbling trains of mental whimsy
Criss-cross wastelands of self-doubt
    Till a vision shuts them out:

Because God borrows your firm arms
To hold me sov'reignly till forms
Of strangely artless idleness
Obey your toughish tenderness
(That understands my foolishness).
Then with puzzled frown you bless
My peace-filled mind with silence deep
Enough to cleanse my soul in sleep.

Sustenance

Your favored presence turned my eyes
From winds of doubting rage that would
Have terrified love-surfaced skies
To hide the lake of peace whereon the good
Of Life awaited with surprise
For willing hearts that venture as they should.

Your fellowship engaged my will to offer
Hymns of courage for new depths unseen.
A lily-pad (God wrought) became my altar
(His symbol of your strength) that lay serene
To rest me after walking on the water.
Now the certainties of land are lean.

Sweet Tomorrows

Sweet Tomorrows, tho' shouldst with-hold
The new from me (who am so new to Time),
No lesser melody should claim my rhyme.
For I have Today—
And Yesterdays still as fresh
As thy deeply sleeping rose
Of promise. And my day surely knows
This quietude my loves design—
Whilst Thou, Sweet Morrows, only pine.

Reflections on the Iris

With tender smiles I scan their faces.
They innocently smile at me.
Deep within their purple laces
Thoughts of him are all I see.

Arm in arm their stalks are standing
Tall and resolute and free:
An image of his will demanding
Freedom from my love he sees.

While they merge their full-blown beauty
Reverenced for their flowing grace,
My love still flowers, too, in duty
Seeking courage to embrace

A truth this tenderness must seed
In gardens of Tomorrow's fare
When there'll be a further need
For this love to word my prayer.

My Darkened Heart

The sun won't shine through a darkened heart—
Now that you've told me that we have to part.
You don't know, Darling, just what it means,
You leave me heart-aches and empty dreams.

My darkened heart, Dear, My darkened heart
Is filled with longing for you, Sweetheart.
Though years will lengthen and turn to pain
I'll never turn, Dear, To love again.

My world is lonely and growing cold
Without the joy, Dear, your arms foretold
And gave me haven from worldly cares;
Now I've only memories and prayers.

Love Is Supreme

To love you is to know my need.
Can loneliness avenge my night?
—If God were willing to concede
His gift holds no divine insight!

Love has no rival for its truth.
In self-sufficiency it rests
Pavilioned in its sacred booth
Addressing its own worthiness.

Loverhood

Of all of Earth's perplexing schemes
I'm partial to the breeze that brings
Its musical and soothing themes
On Quietude's unhurried wings.

Last night that breeze from Lebanon
Gave cedared perfume to his hair
And lured a dimpled smile upon
His cheek and left him in my care.

These self-same breezes compassed Stonehenge
And fathomed centuries of seers
To challenge me or to avenge
My joy in dialogue with theirs.

Anon! My view is freshly drawn
From regions newly understood:
His waking eyes revealed my dawn
Of everlasting loverhood.

In Absentia

Your lambent prescience filtered muted strife;
Its truce inhabited my vacant soul,
Carpeting my hills and vales of life
With rainbows of your presence as my gold.

Now your absence like a fear is borne
Through prayed-out night and trembling, holy morn.
The quick'ning beauties caught in mid-day dreams
Mirage their memories in muffled screams.

Through migrant years of omen-laden skies
Remains the solace of your grey-green eyes.
A loyal heart is cast as molten lead
Weighing hard upon an empty bed.

The satin-covered pillow is not warm
Circling my shoulder like an arm
But never reaches with desire to listen
To happenings my daylight hours christen.

By dint of strength my faith has portioned me
My will is ready for this calvary
That nails your absence to its hope. Somehow
It's traditional with me by now.

Tho' Wisdom carve this pain with laser light,
No Burden-Torch shall blind Joy's freedom flight:
Our spirits' long togetherness is true.
My heart will tryst absentia with you.

Holiness

O that my thoughts were holy thoughts!
And the mind could only know
The angel-minted sweeter quaffs
Of life to keep my heart aglow.

But should such wond'rous holiness
Implore my wistful heart define
Some strange unpeopled wholesomeness—
I could not author its design.

Were holiness mere sinlessness
Beyond the hurt of humankind,
Could strife enhance the relevance
Of potent truth and love's tart wine?

An holy thought as clear as light
Became our love: a rainbow bent
To canopy our days and nights
Divining charities well spent.

This holy thought—an art of God—
This porthole of Infinity,
Is but the telescoping of
God's reason for Eternity.

When You Go

Forgive me if the note is gay,
(Why review so sweet a sorrow
Of your going yesterday;
Perchance you will return tomorrow?)

Furthermore there is in store
Melodies my rhyme's concealing
Day by day the song is more
Than its music is revealing.

Be patient with my lingering,
The heart needs dwell upon each Now:
My rosary of days are fingering
The pride of each recurring hour.

Oh hear, Beloved, simply this:
I've bliss to spare, and yet will borrow
Anticipations of your kiss.
(Now is lesser than tomorrow!)

Your Absence

I've loved your absence, Sweet, today,
This strange world your awayness brings.
It gave my heart a new skyway
Thru which to try its restless wings.

Up and up higher still
Than I had ever meant to be
My thoughts winged on and on until
I lost sight of you and memory.

Then my heart was sad to know
Too much newness—lest alone—
I'd lose the joyous afterglow
Of you for compassing me home.

Waiting

However sweet the daylight is—
Sweeter still the glimpse of his
Enduring gentleness that lies
Serenely in his grey-green eyes
That measure raptures of the mind
And savor answers wise men find.

Why does the heart in hunger wander
Fawning through the night to ponder
Tattered patterns to enshrine
Tomorrow's greening hope-held vine
As blooming with ecstasy—
And thus up-root integrity?

Oh, that common daylight see
The power and grandeur love can be.
Filt'ring through a sieve of stars
Lacing moonbeams weave more scars
To shroud my recompense; But wait!
I know his arms as heaven's gate.

Valentine '79

Even in Death

I'll come to you a gentle breeze
And linger softly as a kiss;
Then quietly, like falling leaves
I'll nestle near—unseen unmissed?

Unconditionally—"Yes"

Is my love those quick'ning, transcendental
    Momentary glimpse of your soul?
Are they meant to be the sacramental
    Quaffs of Time imbibing Truth foretold.

Then the heart derives this newly wise
    Annunciation of the native homing
Of Beauty's habitation in your eyes
    And recognition blesses our belonging:

To tranquilities that savor Life
As mysteries awaiting Wisdom's quest
Although it challenges with certain strife:
I'll answer unconditionally, "Yes"!

Your Presence

This canopy aglow with wonderment
Is joy I know because you're standing near me.
To ecstasy this precious hour is lent
For eulogising moments to deter me
Should the music of my song relent.

Perchance this joy must linger underground
To nourish mysteries that heartaches hold
In silent meditation too profound
To squander prematurely sorrow's gold
That gilds the cross and celebrates the crown.

Beside you I'm so newly holy-wise,
Holding thoughts more dear than mere content,
My rose of hope lies tranquil in your eyes
While sterner grace abides to circumvent
The joy-rimmed pain your presence magnifies.

Through Love's Eternity

You're playing on my heartstrings
With eyes of happiness
A melody that angels sing
And bid my soul confess
That life is real as love is true
And truly as I live
Oh, were it not for such as you
I'd have no love to give.

Upon your heart of golden strings
I'll play Life's melody
That we may know our perfect dream
Through love's eternity: through love's eternity.

Ambience

His presence seems a moon-drenched meadow
    Where my heart leaps as the doe
In and out among the heather
    Abandoned to the cresting flow

Of happiness that spans Time's River,
    Clothed with freedom to avow
This presence is the pristine giver
    Of joy-bourne airs to bird and bough.

Tomorrow morning he'll be going:
    His absence spreading o'er the lea
Like an Angelus echoing
    Will candelize a path for me.

Who Is My Love?

Who is my love?
What is his name?
And who calls him so?

Where is he
Today? And how
Shall his voice I know?

The timbre of his soul
Shall speak Life's truth
And I shall feel the pain
Of living and be glad.